Making Math Easy

Subtraction Made Easy

Rebecca Wingard-Nelson

Enslow Elementary
an imprint of
Enslow Publishers, Inc.
40 Industrial Road
Box 398
Berkeley Heights, NJ 07922
USA
PO Box 38
Aldershot
Hants GU12 6BP
UK
http://www.enslow.com

Enslow Elementary, an imprint of Enslow Publishers, Inc.

Library of Congress Cataloging-in-Publication Data

Wingard-Nelson, Rebecca.
Subtraction made easy / Rebecca Wingard-Nelson.
p. cm.— (Making math easy)
Includes index.
ISBN-10: 0-7660-2509-8 (hardcover)
1. Subtraction—Juvenile literature. I. Title.
QA115.W77 2005
513.2'12—dc22

2004021658

ISBN-13: 978-0-7660-2509-7

Printed in the United States of America

10 9 8 7 6 5 4 3

To Our Readers: We have done our best to make sure all Internet Addresses in this book were active and appropriate when we went to press. However, the author and the publisher have no control over and assume no liability for the material available on those Internet sites or on other Web sites they may link to. Any comments or suggestions can be sent by e-mail to comments@enslow.com or to the address on the back cover.

Illustrations: Tom LaBaff

Cover illustration: Tom LaBaff

Contents

Introduction

Math is used everywhere, and it is an important part of your life. You use math when you are playing games, cooking food, spending money, telling time, reading music, and doing any other activity that involves numbers. Even finding a television station uses math!

Subtraction Is Everywhere

You use subtraction all the time and probably never think about it. Every time you find the difference between two values, you are subtracting. When you find how long it took you to do something, you are subtracting time values. When you buy something and receive change, you are subtracting money values. When you have a certain amount of homework to do, and finish part of the problems, you use subtraction to figure out how many you still have left to do.

Using This Book

This book can be used to learn or review subtraction at your own speed. It can be used on your own or with a friend, tutor, or parent. Get ready to discover math . . . made easy!

What I

When you subtract, you take away one number from another number.

If you have seven cookies and you take away (or subtract) two cookies, you will have five cookies left.

$$7 - 2 = 5$$

ubtraction?

Subtraction can tell you the difference between two things. One example is a difference in age between two people.

Jennifer is 8 years old. Her brother Bobby is 3 years old. Use subtraction to find the difference in their ages.

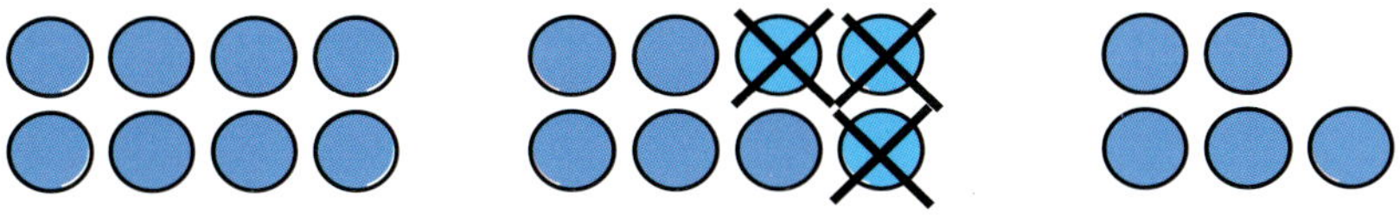

8 years − 3 years = 5 years

The difference between Jennifer's age and Bobby's age is 5 years. So, Jennifer is 5 years older than Bobby.

One-Digi

Here is a list of basic subtraction facts. If you memorize these basic facts, subtracting larger numbers will be easy.

0 − 0 = 0

1 − 0 = 1
1 − 1 = 0

2 − 0 = 2
2 − 1 = 1
2 − 2 = 0

3 − 0 = 3
3 − 1 = 2
3 − 2 = 1
3 − 3 = 0

4 − 0 = 4
4 − 1 = 3
4 − 2 = 2
4 − 3 = 1
4 − 4 = 0

5 − 0 = 5
5 − 1 = 4
5 − 2 = 3
5 − 3 = 2
5 − 4 = 1
5 − 5 = 0

6 − 0 = 6
6 − 1 = 5
6 − 2 = 4
6 − 3 = 3
6 − 4 = 2
6 − 5 = 1
6 − 6 = 0

ubtraction

7 − 0 = 7
7 − 1 = 6
7 − 2 = 5
7 − 3 = 4
7 − 4 = 3
7 − 5 = 2
7 − 6 = 1
7 − 7 = 0

8 − 0 = 8
8 − 1 = 7
8 − 2 = 6
8 − 3 = 5
8 − 4 = 4
8 − 5 = 3
8 − 6 = 2
8 − 7 = 1
8 − 8 = 0

9 − 0 = 9
9 − 1 = 8
9 − 2 = 7
9 − 3 = 6
9 − 4 = 5
9 − 5 = 4
9 − 6 = 3
9 − 7 = 2
9 − 8 = 1
9 − 9 = 0

Subtraction

Subtraction problems can be written in two ways, in a line or in a column.

line	column
$6 - 5 = 1$	$\begin{array}{r} 6 \\ -\ 5 \\ \hline 1 \end{array}$

The subtraction symbol, –, means to subtract, or take away. The symbol is sometimes called the minus sign. The equal sign, =, means equals. Equals means "the same as."

When you read a subtraction problem out loud, you say,

Six minus five equals one.

$$6 \quad - \quad 5 \quad = \quad 1$$

erms

The number you start with in a subtraction problem is called the minuend. The number that is being taken away is called the subtrahend.

$$\begin{array}{rl} 7 & \longleftarrow \text{minuend} \\ -\ 3 & \longleftarrow \text{subtrahend} \\ \hline 4 & \end{array}$$

The answer to a subtraction problem is called the difference.

$$\begin{array}{rl} 7 & \\ -\ 3 & \\ \hline 4 & \longleftarrow \text{difference} \end{array}$$

Addition an

Addition and subtraction are inverse operations. Addition puts values together and subtraction takes values apart.

operation—An actio that works to change a number.
inverse operations—Operations that undo each other.

If you have 7 eggs and add 2 eggs, you will have 9 eggs. If you have 9 eggs and subtract 2 eggs, you have 7 eggs.

ubtraction

You can use subtraction to check the answer to an addition problem.

$$\begin{array}{r} 6 \\ +\ 1 \\ \hline 7 \end{array}$$

The answer to this addition problem is 7. Check the answer by subtracting one of the numbers you added from the sum.

$$\begin{array}{r} 7 \\ -\ 1 \\ \hline 6 \end{array}$$

When the difference is the other number in the addition problem, the sum is correct.

You can use addition to check the answer in a subtraction problem.

$$\begin{array}{r} 9 \\ -\ 3 \\ \hline 6 \end{array}$$

The answer to this subtraction problem is 6.

$$\begin{array}{r} 6 \\ +\ 3 \\ \hline 9 \end{array}$$

Add the answer to the number you subtracted. When the sum is the same as the number you started with, the answer is correct.

Subtraction

When you subtract zero (0) from any other number, the number stays the same.

If you have nine balloons and you take away zero balloons, you still have nine balloons.

nd Zero

The zero property of subtraction is always true, no matter how large the original number.

The Zero Property—
number − 0 =
number

$$\begin{array}{r} 7 \\ -\ 0 \\ \hline 7 \end{array} \qquad \begin{array}{r} 83 \\ -\ 0 \\ \hline 83 \end{array} \qquad \begin{array}{r} 4{,}632 \\ -\ 0 \\ \hline 4{,}632 \end{array}$$

When you subtract a number from itself, the answer is zero.

$$\begin{array}{r} 3 \\ -\ 3 \\ \hline 0 \end{array} \qquad \begin{array}{r} 9 \\ -\ 9 \\ \hline 0 \end{array} \qquad \begin{array}{r} 16 \\ -\ 16 \\ \hline 0 \end{array}$$

$$\begin{array}{r} 87 \\ -\ 87 \\ \hline 0 \end{array} \qquad \begin{array}{r} 1{,}004 \\ -\ 1{,}004 \\ \hline 0 \end{array} \qquad \begin{array}{r} 82{,}563 \\ -\ 82{,}563 \\ \hline 0 \end{array}$$

Subtraction

In addition, you can add two numbers in any order. The order does not change the answer.

$$3 + 2 = 5$$
$$2 + 3 = 5$$

Is this true for subtraction?

$$3 - 2 = 1$$
$$2 - 3 = -1$$

The answers are **not** the same. You **cannot** change the order of the numbers in subtraction.

roperties

When you add three or more numbers, you can group them in any way. Grouping does not change the answer.

Add or subtract numbers inside the parentheses first.

$$(4 + 3) + 1 = (7) + 1 = 8$$
$$4 + (3 + 1) = 4 + (4) = 8$$

Is this true for subtraction?

$$(4 - 3) - 1 = (1) - 1 = 0$$
$$4 - (3 - 1) = 4 - (2) = 2$$

The answers are **not** the same. In subtraction, you **cannot** group the numbers in any way.

Plac

All numbers are written using these ten symbols, called digits.

0, 1, 2, 3, 4, 5, 6, 7, 8, 9

Numbers that are less than ten use only one digit. Larger numbers use more digits.

The number 253 has three digits, each in a different place. Each place has its own value.

alue

hundreds tens ones

2 5 3

In the number 253, the digit **3** is in the ones place.
That means the digit has a value of 3 ones.

The digit **5** is in the tens place.
It has a value of 5 tens.

The digit **2** is in the hundreds place.
It has a value of 2 hundreds.

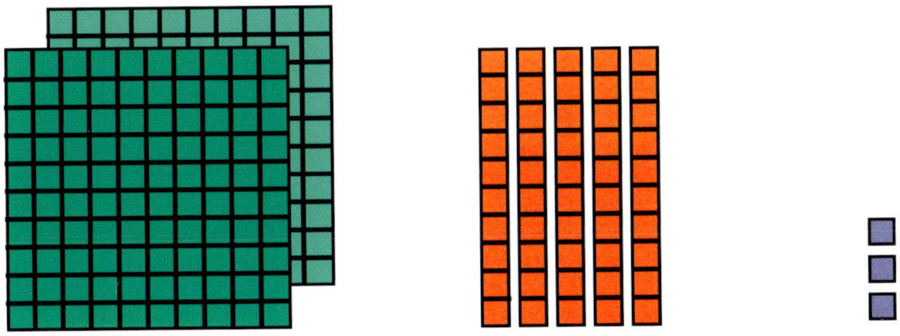

2 hundreds (200) + 5 tens (50) + 3 ones (3)

253

Two-Digi

Two-digit numbers are subtracted using place value. Write two-digit subtraction problems in columns. Write the numbers so that the same place values are lined up.

tens	ones	
5	1	51 is the same as 5 tens and 1 one.
− 2	0	20 is the same as 2 tens and 0 ones.

Begin by subtracting in the ones place. Write the difference of the ones in the ones place of the answer.

$$\begin{array}{r} 51 \\ -\ 20 \\ \hline 1 \end{array}$$

Now subtract in the tens place. Write the difference of the tens in the tens place of the answer.

$$\begin{array}{r} 51 \\ -\ 20 \\ \hline 31 \end{array}$$

$$51 - 20 = 31$$

ubtraction

Let's look at another problem.

$$\begin{array}{r} 78 \\ -\ 35 \\ \hline \end{array} \qquad \begin{array}{r} 78 \\ -\ 35 \\ \hline 3 \end{array} \qquad \begin{array}{r} 78 \\ -\ 35 \\ \hline 43 \end{array}$$

Regrouping

Sometimes the number you are subtracting in a column is larger than the number above it.

$$\begin{array}{r} 32 \\ -\ \ 7 \\ \hline \end{array}$$

7 is greater than 2. There are not enough ones in 32 to subtract 7 ones.

You can regroup.

The number 32 is 3 tens and 2 ones.

3 tens + 2 ones

You can regroup 32 by changing 1 ten into 10 ones.

2 tens + 12 ones

The regrouped 12 ones are now greater than the 7 ones, so you can subtract.

Numbers

Let's look at another regrouping. How can you regroup 50?

You can group 50 as 5 tens and 0 ones.

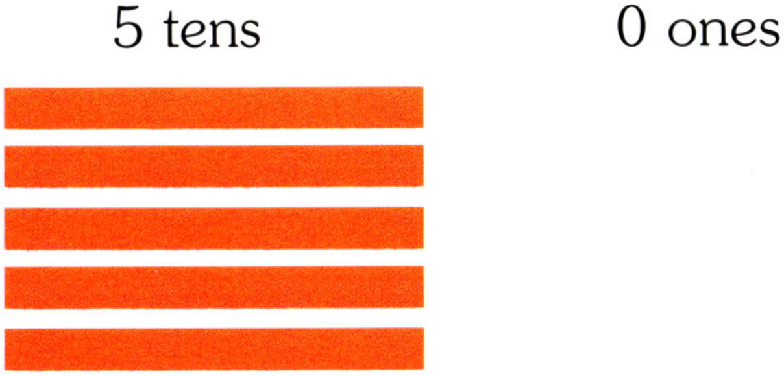

You can regroup 50 by changing 1 ten into 10 ones.

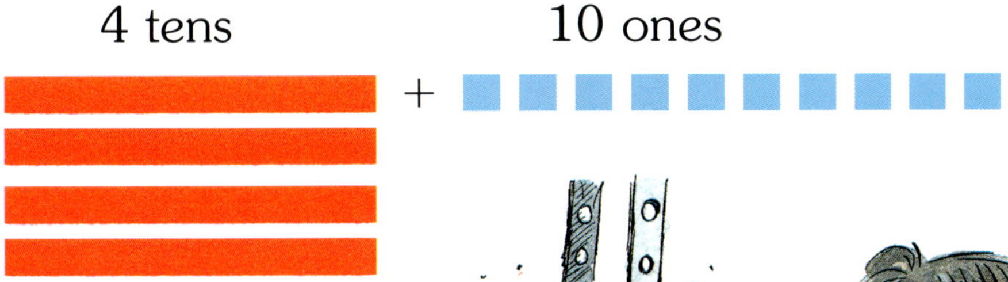

Two-Digi

Let's solve the problem we regrouped on page 22.

$$\begin{array}{r} 32 \\ -\ \ 7 \\ \hline \end{array}$$

$$\begin{array}{r} {\scriptstyle 2\ 12} \\ \not{3}\not{2} \\ -\ \ 7 \\ \hline \end{array}$$

How do you regroup? Take 1 ten from the tens place. 3 − 1 = 2. There are now 2 tens. Cross out the 3 and write a 2 above it. Regroup the ten as 10 ones. 2 ones + 10 ones = 12 ones. There are now 12 ones. Cross out the 2 and write 12 above it.

$$\begin{array}{r} {\scriptstyle 2\ 12} \\ \not{3}\not{2} \\ -\ \ 7 \\ \hline 5 \end{array}$$

Subtract in the ones place.
12 − 7 = 5
Write a 5 in the ones place.

$$\begin{array}{r} {\scriptstyle 2\ 12} \\ \not{3}\not{2} \\ -\ \ 7 \\ \hline 25 \end{array}$$

Subtract in the tens place. There is no number to be subtracted in the tens place. 2 − 0 = 2
Write a 2 in the tens place.

egrouping

Let's do another.

$$\begin{array}{r} 50 \\ -\ 38 \\ \hline \end{array}$$

In the ones place, 8 is greater than 0. You need to regroup.

$$\begin{array}{r} \overset{4}{\cancel{5}}\overset{10}{\cancel{0}} \\ -\ 38 \\ \hline \end{array}$$

Take 1 ten from the tens place. 5 − 1 = 4. Cross out the 5 and write 4 above it. Regroup the ten as 10 ones. 0 + 10 = 10. Cross out the 0 and write 10 above it.

$$\begin{array}{r} \overset{4}{\cancel{5}}\overset{10}{\cancel{0}} \\ -\ 38 \\ \hline 2 \end{array}$$

Subtract in the ones place.

10 − 8 = 2

Write a 2 in the ones place.

$$\begin{array}{r} \overset{4}{\cancel{5}}\overset{10}{\cancel{0}} \\ -\ 38 \\ \hline 12 \end{array}$$

Subtract the tens.

4 − 3 = 1

Write a 1 in the tens place.

Three-Digi

Subtracting three-digit numbers is just like subtracting two-digit numbers.

$$724 - 204$$

$$\begin{array}{r} 724 \\ -\ 204 \\ \hline \end{array}$$

Write the numbers in columns.
Line up the place values.

Always subtract from right to left.

$$\begin{array}{r} 724 \\ -\ 204 \\ \hline 0 \end{array}$$

Subtract in the ones place.
$4 - 4 = 0$
Write a 0 in the ones place.

$$\begin{array}{r} 724 \\ -\ 204 \\ \hline 20 \end{array}$$

Subtract in the tens place.
$2 - 0 = 2$
Write a 2 in the tens place.

$$\begin{array}{r} 724 \\ -\ 204 \\ \hline 520 \end{array}$$

Subtract in the hundreds place.
$7 - 2 = 5$
Write a 5 in the hundreds place.

ubtraction

Let's do another.

$$\begin{array}{r} 682 \\ -\ 630 \\ \hline \end{array} \quad \begin{array}{r} 682 \\ -\ 630 \\ \hline 2 \end{array} \quad \begin{array}{r} 682 \\ -\ 630 \\ \hline 52 \end{array} \quad \begin{array}{r} 682 \\ -\ 630 \\ \hline 52 \end{array}$$

The difference in the hundreds place is zero. $6 - 6 = 0$. When the difference in the farthest left place is zero, leave the place blank.

Three-Digi

When you need a larger value in the tens place, you can regroup the hundreds place. Regroup 1 hundred as 10 tens.

$$468 - 181$$

$$\begin{array}{r} 468 \\ -\ 181 \\ \hline \end{array}$$

Write the numbers in columns.
Line up the place values.

$$\begin{array}{r} 468 \\ -\ 181 \\ \hline 7 \end{array}$$

Subtract in the ones place.
$8 - 1 = 7$
Write a 7 in the ones place.

$$\begin{array}{r} {\scriptstyle 3\ 16} \\ \not{4}\not{6}8 \\ -\ 181 \\ \hline 7 \end{array}$$

In the tens place, the 8 is larger than the 6, so regroup 1 hundred as 10 tens. Add 10 tens to the 6 ten. $10 + 6 = 16$ tens.

3 16
~~4~~~~6~~8
− 181
87

Subtract in the tens place.

16 − 8 = 8

Write an 8 in the tens place.

3 16
~~4~~~~6~~8
− 181
287

Subtract in the hundreds place.

3 − 1 = 2

Write a 2 in the hundreds place.

Greate

Numbers that have more than three digits are subtracted the same way as smaller numbers. Subtract one place value at a time from right to left.

2,590 − 1,410

$$\begin{array}{r} 2{,}590 \\ -\ 1{,}410 \\ \hline \end{array}$$

Write the numbers in columns. Line up the place values.

$$\begin{array}{r} 2{,}590 \\ -\ 1{,}410 \\ \hline 0 \end{array}$$

Subtract in the ones place.

0 − 0 = 0

Write a 0 in the ones place.

$$\begin{array}{r} 2{,}590 \\ -\ 1{,}410 \\ \hline 80 \end{array}$$

Subtract in the tens place.

9 − 1 = 8

Write an 8 in the tens place.

$$\begin{array}{r} 2{,}590 \\ -\ 1{,}410 \\ \hline 180 \end{array}$$

Subtract in the hundreds place.

5 − 4 = 1

Write a 1 in the hundreds place.

$$\begin{array}{r} 2{,}590 \\ -\ 1{,}410 \\ \hline 1{,}180 \end{array}$$

Subtract in the thousands place.

2 − 1 = 1

Write a 1 in the thousands place.

$$2{,}590 - 1{,}410 = 1{,}180$$

Regroupin

Regrouping can be used with any place value and as often as necessary.

$$\begin{array}{r} 4\ 11 \\ 4{,}0\not{5}\not{1} \\ -\ 3{,}922 \\ \hline 9 \end{array}$$

The 2 is larger than the 1, so regroup 1 ten as 10 ones. Subtract in the ones place. $11 - 2 = 9$

$$\begin{array}{r} 4\ 11 \\ 4{,}0\not{5}\not{1} \\ -\ 3{,}922 \\ \hline 29 \end{array}$$

Subtract in the tens place.
$4 - 2 = 2$

$$\begin{array}{r} 3\ 10\ 4\ 11 \\ \not{4}{,}\not{0}\not{5}\not{1} \\ -\ 3{,}922 \\ \hline 129 \end{array}$$

Subtract in the hundreds place. Regroup 1 thousand as 10 hundreds.
$10 - 9 = 1$

$$\begin{array}{r} 3\ 10\ 4\ 11 \\ \not{4}{,}\not{0}\not{5}\not{1} \\ -\ 3{,}922 \\ \hline 129 \end{array}$$

Subtract in the thousands.
$3 - 3 = 0$ This is the farthest place left, so leave it blank.

Let's do another.

$$2{,}394 - 807$$

$$\begin{array}{r} {}^{8\,14} \\ 2{,}394 \\ -\ \ 807 \\ \hline 7 \end{array} \qquad \begin{array}{r} {}^{8\,14} \\ 2{,}394 \\ -\ \ 807 \\ \hline 87 \end{array} \qquad \begin{array}{r} {}^{1\,13\,8\,14} \\ 2{,}394 \\ -\ \ 807 \\ \hline 587 \end{array} \qquad \begin{array}{r} {}^{1\,13\,8\,14} \\ 2{,}394 \\ -\ \ 807 \\ \hline 1587 \end{array}$$

Rounding T

Sometimes you only need to know an estimate, instead of an exact answer. For example, if you had $842 and spent $593, about how much would you have left? You want an estimate of the amount of money you have left.

estimate—An answer that is not exact; a reasonable guess.

One way to estimate the answer is to round each number to the greatest place value. The greatest place value for 842 and 593 is the hundreds place. To estimate to the hundreds place, see if the number in the tens place is greater, equal to, or less than 5.

593 has a 9 in the tens place. The digit 9 is 5 or more. 593 is closer to 600 than to 500. Round 593 to 600.

842 has a 4 in the tens place. The digit 4 is less than 5. 842 is closer to 800 than to 900. Round 842 to 800.

stimate

Estimate 842 − 593.

842 rounds to 800
593 rounds to 600

$$\begin{array}{r} 800 \\ -\ 600 \\ \hline 200 \end{array}$$

The estimated difference of 842 − 593 is 200.
You have about $200 left.

You can also estimate by rounding to a smaller place value.

Estimate 689 − 133 to the tens place.

689 rounded to the tens place is 690.
133 rounded to the tens place is 130.

$$\begin{array}{r} 690 \\ -\ 130 \\ \hline 560 \end{array}$$

The estimated difference of 689 − 133 is 560.

Estimation vs

Rounding to a smaller place value gives a closer estimate than rounding to a larger place value.

A. Estimate 637 − 82 to the hundreds place.

Write the numbers in columns. Round each to the nearest hundreds.

$$\begin{array}{rl} 637 & \text{rounds to } 600 \\ -\ \ 82 & \text{rounds to } 100 \\ \hline \end{array}$$

Subtract.

$$\begin{array}{r} 600 \\ -\ 100 \\ \hline 500 \end{array}$$

B. Estimate 637 − 82 to the tens place.

Write the numbers in columns. Round each to the nearest tens.

$$\begin{array}{rl} 637 & \text{rounds to } 640 \\ -\ \ 82 & \text{rounds to } 80 \\ \hline \end{array}$$

xact Difference

Subtract. Regroup
1 hundred as 10 tens.

```
 5 14
 6 4 0
-  8 0
 -----
 5 6 0
```

C. Find the exact difference.

```
 5 13
 6 3 7
-  8 2
 -----
 5 5 5
```

Rounding to the tens place gives you a closer estimate than rounding to the hundreds place.

Exact difference:
555
Rounding to tens:
560
Rounding to hundreds:
500

Menta

Problems that don't need regrouping can be done mentally by subtracting one place value at a time.

$$85 - 31$$

In the ones place, subtract 1 from 5. $5 - 1 = 4$.
In the tens place, subtract 3 from 8. $8 - 3 = 5$.

$$85 - 31 = 54$$

ubtraction

Some subtraction problems can be solved mentally by changing the problem. In subtraction, you can add or subtract the same number from **both numbers** without changing the answer.

$11 - 8 = 3$

+2 ↓ +2 ↓

$13 - 10 = 3$

The answers are the same.

By changing the second number to a number that ends in a zero, the problem can more easily be solved mentally.

$$56 - 29$$

You can change 29 to 30 by adding 1. If you mentally add one to each number, this problem becomes easy.

$56 - 29 = ?$

+1 ↓ +1 ↓

$57 - 30 = 27$, so $56 - 29 = 27$

Subtractin

When you subtract time values, always subtract the same units. Hours are subtracted from hours, and days are subtracted from days.

There are 3 weeks and 6 days of summer vacation left. You are going to spend 2 weeks and 2 days at your aunt's house. How much vacation time will be left after your visit with your aunt?

Always subtract from right to left, smallest units first.

Subtract days first.

	3 weeks 6 days
−	2 weeks 2 days
	4 days

Subtract weeks.

	3 weeks 6 days
−	2 weeks 2 days
	1 week 4 days

You will have 1 week and 4 days left.

ime

Let's do one that uses hours and minutes.

12 hours 37 minutes − 6 hours 16 minutes

Subtract minutes first.

	12 hours 37 minutes
−	6 hours 16 minutes
	21 minutes

Subtract hours.

	12 hours 37 minutes
−	6 hours 16 minutes
	6 hours 21 minutes

Subtraction

Look at the question "You have 9 oranges. How many oranges will be left when you take away 2?" The words *left* and *take away* tell you that you should subtract.

9 oranges − 2 oranges = 7 oranges

Words that help you know how to solve problems are called key words. Some key words for subtraction problems are listed in the table below.

Subtraction Key Words		
changed	fewer than	reduced
compared to	left	remain
decreased by	less than	smaller
difference	lost	subtract
dropped	minus	take away

ey Words

Use the key words to change a word problem into a math problem.

Jane's class had an ice cream party. They started with 8 quarts of ice cream. They ate 6 quarts of ice cream. How much ice cream was left after the party?

The word "left" tells you to subtract.

8 quarts − 6 quarts = 2 quarts

There were 2 quarts of ice cream left after the party.

Wor

There are four steps to problem solving. You use these steps every day in real life.

Last week, Kathleen's score on a certain video game was 32,000 points. This week she didn't have time to play very often, and her score decreased by 4,000 points. What is her score this week?

roblems

Understand the problem. Find what you know (score last week) and what you want to know (score this week).

Decide how you can solve the problem. The key words *decreased by* tell you that you can use subtraction to solve the problem.

Solve the problem. Subtract the number of points the score was decreased by from last week's score.

$$\begin{array}{rl} 32{,}000 & \text{score last week} \\ -\ \ \underline{4{,}000} & \text{decrease in score} \\ 28{,}000 & \text{score this week} \end{array}$$

Check your work. Make sure you have answered the right question. Remember, you can use addition to check your subtraction.

$$28{,}000 + 4{,}000 = 32{,}000$$

Further Reading

Cato, Sheila, and Sami Sweeten. *Subtraction*. Minneapolis: Carolrhoda Books, 1999.

Creative Teaching Press. *Addition and Subtraction Facts to 20*. Santa Barbara, Calif.: Creative Teaching Press, 2002.

Leedy, Loreen. *Subtraction Action*. New York: Holiday House, 2000.

Skinner, Daphne, and John A. Nez. *Tightwad Tod*. New York: Disney Press, 2001.

Internet Addresses

Banfill, J. *AAA Math.* "Subtraction." © 2000–2002.
<http://www.aaamath.com/sub.html>

Dell, Diana. *Gamequarium.* "Subtraction Games."
<http://www.gamequarium.com/subtraction.html>

The Math Forum. *Ask Dr Math.* "Ask Dr. Math." © 1994–2004.
<http://mathforum.org/library/drmath/sets/elem_subtraction.html>

Index